D1466282

Introducción a los padres

We Both Read es la primera serie de libros diseñada para invitar a padres e hijos a compartir la lectura de un cuento, por turnos y en voz alta. Esta "lectura compartida" —que se ha desarrollado en conjunto con especialistas en primeras lecturas— invita a los padres a leer los textos más complejos en la página de la izquierda. Luego, les toca a los niños leer las páginas de la derecha, que contienen textos más sencillos, escritos específicamente para primeros lectores.

Leer en voz alta es una de las actividades más importantes que los padres comparten con sus hijos para ayudarlos a desarrollar la lectura. Sin embargo, *We Both Read* no es solo leerle *a* un niño, sino que les permite a los padres leer *con* el niño. *We Both Read* es más poderoso y efectivo porque combina dos elementos claves del aprendizaje: "demostración" (el padre lee) y "aplicación" (el niño lee). El resultado no es solo que el niño aprende a leer más rápido, ¡sino que ambos disfrutan y se enriquecen con esta experiencia!

Sería más útil si usted lee el libro completo y en voz alta la primera vez, y luego invita a su niño a participar en una segunda lectura. En algunos libros, las palabras más difíciles se presentan por primera vez en **negritas** en el texto del padre. Señalar o hablar sobre estas palabras ayudará a su niño a familiarizarse con ellas y a ampliar su vocabulario. También notará que el ícono "lee el padre" ☺ precede el texto del padre y el ícono "lee el niño" ☺ precede el texto del niño.

Lo invitamos a compartir y a relacionarse con su niño mientras leen el libro juntos. Si su hijo tiene dificultad, usted puede mencionar algunas cosas que lo ayuden. "Decir cada sonido" es bueno, pero puede que esto no funcione con todas las palabras. Los niños pueden hallar pistas en las palabras del cuento, en el contexto de las oraciones e incluso en las imágenes. Algunos cuentos incluyen patrones y rimas que los ayudarán. También le podría ser útil a su niño tocar las palabras con su dedo mientras lee, para conectar mejor el sonido de la voz con la palabra impresa.

¡Al compartir los libros de *We Both Read*, usted y su hijo vivirán juntos la fascinante aventura de la lectura! Es una manera divertida y fácil de animar y ayudar a su niño a leer —¡y una maravillosa manera de preparar a su niño para disfrutar de la lectura durante toda su vida!

Parent's Introduction

We Both Read is the first series of books designed to invite parents and children to share the reading of a story by taking turns reading aloud. This "shared reading" innovation, which was developed with reading education specialists, invites parents to read the more complex text and story line on the left-hand pages. Then, children can be encouraged to read the right-hand pages, which feature text written for a specific early reading level.

Reading aloud is one of the most important activities parents can share with their child to assist them in their reading development. However, *We Both Read* goes beyond reading to a child and allows parents to share the reading with a child. *We Both Read* is so powerful and effective because it combines two key elements in learning: "modeling" (the parent reads) and "doing" (the child reads). The result is not only faster reading development for the child, but a much more enjoyable and enriching experience for both!

You may find it helpful to read the entire book aloud yourself the first time, then invite your child to participate in the second reading. In some books, a few more difficult words will first be introduced in the parent's text, distinguished with bold lettering. Pointing out, and even discussing, these words will help familiarize your child with them and help to build your child's vocabulary. Also, note that a "talking parent" icon ☺ precedes the parent's text, and a "talking child" icon ☺ precedes the child's text.

We encourage you to share and interact with your child as you read the book together. If your child is having difficulty, you might want to mention a few things to help him. "Sounding out" is good, but it will not work with all words. Children can pick up clues about the words they are reading from the story, the context of the sentence, or even the pictures. Some stories have rhyming patterns that might help. It might also help them to touch the words with their finger as they read, to better connect the voice sound and the printed word.

Sharing the *We Both Read* books together will engage you and your child in an interactive adventure in reading! It is a fun and easy way to encourage and help your child to read—and a wonderful way to start them off on a lifetime of reading enjoyment!

Zoo Day
A We Both Read® Book:
Level 1

Día del zoológico
Un libro de *We Both Read*:
Nivel 1

Text Copyright © 2012, 2015, 2016 by Treasure Bay, Inc.
By Bruce Johnson and Sindy McKay
Illustrations Copyright © 2012 by Meredith Johnson

This book is based in part on a We Read Phonics book, *A Day at the Zoo*, but it has been significantly expanded and adapted for the We Both Read shared-reading format. You may find the We Read Phonics version to be a complementary and helpful companion to this title.

Reading Consultant: Bruce Johnson, M.Ed.
Translation Services by Cambridge BrickHouse, Inc.
Spanish translation © 2016 by Treasure Bay, Inc.

Published by
Treasure Bay, Inc.
P.O. Box 119
Novato, CA 94948 USA

Printed in Malaysia

Library of Congress Catalog Card Number: 2015940402

ISBN: 978-1-60115-078-3

Visit us online at: www.TreasureBayBooks.com

PR 11-15

WE BOTH READ®

Zoo Day
Día del zoológico

By Bruce Johnson and Sindy McKay

With illustrations by Meredith Johnson

Spanish translation by Yanitzia Canetti

TREASURE BAY

The sun is out and it's a beautiful day to be outside. What can you do?

Sale el sol y es un hermoso día para estar afuera. ¿Qué puedes hacer?

🗣 You can go to the zoo!

¡Puedes ir al zoológico!

You might start by visiting some big animals, like giraffes and **polar bears**. Giraffes don't mind when it's hot outside.

*Puedes comenzar visitando algunos animales grandes, como las jirafas y los **osos polares**. A las jirafas no les importa si hay calor afuera.*

🔊 **Polar bears** *like it to be cold.*

*A los **osos polares** les gustaría que hubiera frío.*

A hippopotamus, or a **hippo**, has very little hair on its body. To protect its bare skin from the hot sun, it spends much of its time in the water.

*Un **hipopótamo** tiene muy poco pelo en su cuerpo. Para proteger su piel desnuda del calor del sol, este pasa gran parte de su tiempo dentro del agua.*

A mother **hippo** takes care
of her pup.

La mamá *hipopótamo* cuida
a su cría.

The biggest animal in the zoo is the African elephant. It is the largest land animal on Earth. It has very large ears. This zoo also has some **smaller** Asian elephants.

*El animal más grande del zoológico es el elefante africano. Es el animal terrestre más grande de la Tierra. Tiene orejas muy grandes. Este zoológico también tiene algunos elefantes asiáticos **más pequeños**.*

They are **smaller** in size and have **smaller** ears.

*Son **más pequeños** de tamaño y tienen orejas **más pequeñas.***

As you walk through the zoo, you might hear a loud roar. That could mean you're getting close to the **lion** enclosure. A **lion**'s roar can be heard from five miles away!

*Mientras caminas por el zoológico, puede que escuches un fuerte rugido. Tal vez eso quiere decir que te estás acercando al foso de los **leones**. ¡El rugido de un león puede escucharse a cinco millas de distancia!*

Lions are very big. Tigers are even bigger!

*Los **leones** son muy grandes. Los tigres son aún más grandes!*

Lions, tigers, and panthers are often called the "big cats." There may also be some smaller types of wild cats in the zoo. One smaller cat is the **serval**.

*A los leones, los tigres y las panteras se les suele llamar "grandes felinos". Puede que también hayan algunos tipos más pequeños de felinos salvajes en el zoológico. El felino más pequeño es el **serval**.*

A **serval** has big ears and long legs. These help him to hunt.

*El **serval** tiene las orejas grandes y las patas largas. Esto lo ayuda a cazar.*

Be sure to visit the giant panda exhibit, where you can watch pandas eat. Giant pandas spend about 12 hours a day eating **bamboo** shoots, stems, and leaves.

*No dejes de visitar la exhibición del panda gigante, donde puedes ver a los pandas comer. Los pandas gigantes pasan cerca de 12 horas al día comiendo brotes de **bambú**, tallos, y hojas.*

Some people eat **bamboo** too. Do you?

*Algunas personas también comen **bambú**. ¿Y tú?*

People often call chimps the "clowns of the zoo." They seem to enjoy goofing around and **smiling** for the camera.

*La gente suele llamar a los chimpancés "los payasos del zoológico". Ellos parecen disfrutar haciendo el tonto y **sonriendo** para la cámara.*

This chimp has a big **smile**!

*¡Este chimpancé tiene una gran **sonrisa**!*

Some zoos have a special house just for birds called an *aviary*. The roof is very high to give the birds plenty of room to fly.

Algunos zoológicos tienen una casa especial para pájaros llamada aviario. El techo es muy alto para darles suficiente espacio para volar.

Most birds can fly. Some birds can also swim.

La mayoría de las aves pueden volar. Algunas también pueden nadar.

There are over ten thousand bird species, from tiny hummingbirds to giant ostriches. A zoo can't house them all. This zoo has a pair of pretty cockatoos. It also has a hawk.

Hay más de diez mil especies de aves, desde diminutos colibríes hasta avestruces gigantes. Un zoológico no puede albergar a todos. Este zoológico tiene un par de lindas cacatúas. También dispone de un halcón.

 This hawk is on the lookout. What do you think it sees?

Este halcón está al acecho. ¿Qué crees que está mirando?

Visiting an exhibit of **insects**, spiders, and scorpions can be creepy and fun. Many **insects** protect themselves from predators by blending into their surroundings.

*Visitar una exhibición de **insectos**, arañas, y escorpiones puede ser espeluznante y divertido. Muchos **insectos** se protegen de los depredadores al confundirse con su entorno.*

This **insect** looks like a stick.
Can you find it?

*Este **insecto** parece un palo.*
¿Puedes encontrarlo?

Scorpions are in the same animal class as **spiders**. A scorpion has a stinger in its tail that injects venom into its prey.

*Los escorpiones están en la misma categoría de animales que las **arañas**. Un escorpión tiene un aguijón en su cola que inyecta veneno a su presa.*

An insect has six legs. A **spider** has eight legs.

*Un insecto tiene seis patas. Una **araña** tiene ocho patas.*

The **reptile** area includes critters that crawl and coil and creep. Some **reptiles**, like this monitor lizard, stay hot in one spot.

*El área **reptil** incluye criaturas que se arrastran y se enroscan y se deslizan. Algunos **reptiles**, como este lagarto monitor, se mantienen calientes en un solo lugar.*

Some **reptiles** stay cool in a pool.

*Algunos **reptiles** se mantienen fríos en un estanque.*

 Crocodiles, alligators, turtles, snakes, and lizards are all reptiles. Some kids are afraid of them.

Los cocodrilos, los caimanes, las tortugas, las serpientes, y los lagartos son reptiles. Algunos niños les tienen miedo.

Some kids love reptiles!

¡A algunos niños les encantan los reptiles!

This zoo has animals from the sea too. This is a manatee, sometimes called a "sea cow." In the pool next door are sea lions and seals. They make a loud **sound**.

*Este zoológico cuenta también con animales marinos. Este es un manatí, a veces llamado "vaca marina". En la piscina de al lado están los lobos marinos y las focas. Producen un fuerte **sonido**.*

Seals bark, but they do not **sound** like dogs.

*Las focas ladran, pero no producen el mismo **sonido** que los perros.*

There is a great variety of animals in the zoo. This zoo has two different kinds of **penguins**. These little guys are rockhopper **penguins**. They are only about one and a half feet tall.

*Hay una gran variedad de animales en el zoológico. Este zoológico tiene dos tipos diferentes de **pingüinos**. Estos chicuelos son **pingüinos** de penacho amarillo. Miden solo un pie y medio de altura.*

These are king **penguins**. They can grow to be three feet tall.

*Estos son los **pingüinos** emperadores. Pueden llegar a medir tres pies de altura.*

 You might be able to visit a special area where you can pet some of the animals. Here you may find sheep, llamas, goats, and other tame animals.

Tal vez puedas visitar un área especial donde puedes acariciar a algunos de los animales. Ahí puedes hallar ovejas, llamas, cabras, y otros animales domésticos.

You can also feed the animals.
Yum, yum!

*También puedes alimentar a
los animales. ¡Qué rico!*

Taking care of so many animals is a big job! It takes many **zookeepers** to keep them all well fed and to clean their habitats.

*¡El cuidado de tantos animales conlleva un gran trabajo! Se necesitan muchos **cuidadores** para mantener a todos bien alimentados y para limpiar sus hábitats.*

The **zookeepers** clean the animals too.

*Los **cuidadores** también bañan a los animales.*

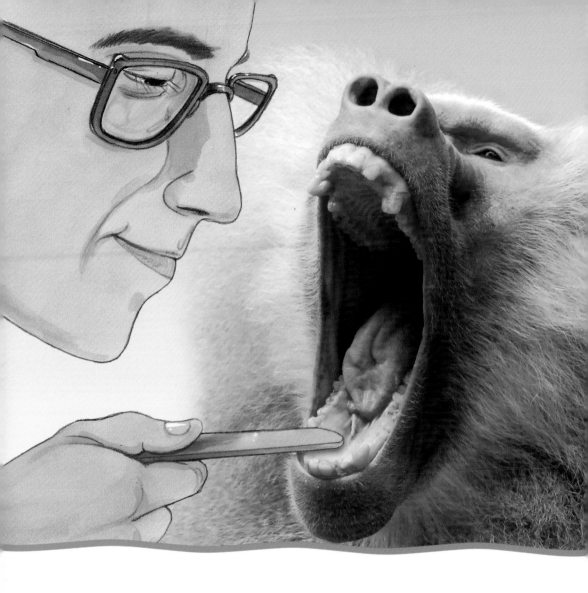

There are also zoo veterinarians who help keep the animals **healthy** and strong. The vets must take care of the animals' teeth and gums.

*También hay veterinarios del zoológico que ayudan a mantener a los animales **sanos** y fuertes. Los veterinarios deben cuidar los dientes y las encías de los animales.*

Vets help the animals in the zoo to stay **healthy**. Baby animals often need extra care.

*Los veterinarios ayudan a los animales del zoológico a estar **sanos**. Las crías suelen necesitar mayores cuidados.*

The zoo is a fun place to see animals and learn many things about them too. So the next time you want to **spend** a day outside, why not go and visit the animals?

*El zoológico es un lugar divertido para ver animales y también para aprender muchas cosas acerca de ellos. Así que la próxima vez que quieras **pasar** un día al aire libre, ¿por qué no hacerles una visita a los animales?*

It is fun to **spend** a day at the zoo!

¡Qué divertido es *pasar* un día en el zoológico!

If you liked **Zoo Day**, here is another
We Both Read® book you are sure to enjoy!

*Si te gustó **Día del zoológico**, ¡seguramente disfrutarás
este otro libro de la serie We Both Read®!*

Amazing Eggs
Huevos asombrosos

Enter the fascinating world of eggs and hatchlings! Birds hatch from eggs, and so do reptiles, amphibians, fish, and insects. Even dinosaurs came from eggs! Look inside and learn about some of the most amazing animals on the planet and how they begin their lives—hatching from an egg.

¡Entra al fascinante mundo de los huevos y las crías! Las aves nacen de huevos, y también los reptiles, anfibios, peces e insectos. ¡Incluso los dinosaurios vinieron de los huevos! Échale un vistazo al libro y aprende sobre algunos de los animales más increíbles del planeta y la forma en que comienzan su vida: la eclosión de un huevo.

To see all the We Both Read books that are available,
just go online to **www.WeBothRead.com**.

*Para ver todos los libros disponibles de la serie We Both Read®,
visita nuestra página web: **www.TreasureBayBooks.com**.*